PIANO • VOCAL • GUITAR

THE Smokey Robinson COLLECTION

CONTENTS

ISBN 0-634-02796-4

7777 W. Bluemound Rd. P.O. Box 13819 Milwaukee,

Visit Hal Leonard Online at
www.halleonard.com

BABY THAT'S BACKATCHA

Words and Music by
WILLIAM "SMOKEY" ROBINSON

Dm9
at - cha, oh ___ yeah, oh ___ yeah,
at - cha, uh ___ huh, oh, ___ ba - by,
ba-by, that's the same thing _ you do for me, _
ba-by, that's back - at - cha, uh - huh, uh ___
ba-by, that's back - at - cha, mm - hmm mm, ___ hmm
oh, ba-by, that's
Fmaj7
Em7
Am
D
1
tit for tat, ___ I'm giv - in' you this for that, ___ ah, ___ oh. ___
2
oh. ___ Ba-by, that's back -

Dm9

at - cha, yeah ___ ba-by, that's the same thing _ you do for me ___
at - cha, back _ at you, ___ ba - by, ___ that's the same thing _ you do for me ___

___ ba-by, that's back - at - cha, Oh, ba-by, that's
___ oh, ___ ba-by, that's back - at - cha, uh - huh, oh ___ ba - by, ___ Oh, ba-by, that's

To Coda

tit for tat, ___ you'd bet-ter be-lieve that I'm gon-na give you this for that, _ oh. _
tit for tat, ___ you'd bet-ter be-lieve that I'm gon-na give you this for that, _ oh. _

Play 3 times

___ Ba-by, that's back - at - cha. Ba-by, that's back -

Fmaj7
Em7
Am
D(add2)
at you.
A touch of
Fmaj7
Em7
Dm7
Fmaj7
Em7
ooh
and some
oh,
ba - by, yeah,
what it is
ex-act - ly
you
Dm7
Fmaj7
Em7
Dm7
don't know, but it is;
so when you feel it, don't
try to con-ceal it, no,
Fmaj7
Em7
E7
D.S. al Coda
just let it hap - pen
for you,
oh,
oh,
ooh.
Ba-by, that's back -

CODA
Dm9
If it makes you feel real good, ba-by that's back - at - cha, make your heart and
soul feel good, ba-by, that's back - at - cha, oh ba-by that's back - at - cha. Ev-'ry-thing I
do just so you can feel good, you know, ba-by that's back - at - cha, ba-by that's back -
at-cha. Ba-by, that's back at you.
Play 4 times
Fmaj7
Em7
Am
D6/9
4fr

BEING WITH YOU

Words and Music by
WILLIAM "SMOKEY" ROBINSON

* Optional repeat of 8 bar Intro. (Instr. solo) before 2nd Verse.

Abmaj7
Fm7
Abmaj7
Fm7
Abmaj7
Gm7
tell me you'll love me and then let me go. I heard the warn-
want it so much 'til it's all in my mind? One thing I know
Cm7
Abmaj7
ing voice from friends and my re - la - tions; they tell me all
for sure is real - ly, real - ly real; I nev - er felt
Bb
1st time D.S.
2nd time D.S. al Coda
a - bout your heart - break rep - u - ta - tion.
be - fore the way you make me feel.
Coda
Cm7
Ebmaj7
Cm7
Repeat ad lib and fade
(lead vocal ad lib)
with you, be - ing with you; be - ing with you:

CRUISIN'

Words and Music by WILLIAM "SMOKEY" ROBINSON
and MARVIN TARPLIN

E
F♯m7
E
one night stand, baby, yeah, so let the music take your
part of each other, ooh baby, yes. Let the music take your
stay there inside you and love you, baby. Let the music take your
F♯m7
E
F♯m7
mind, ooh.
mind. Just release and you will find:
mind.
E
A
D
B
You're gonna fly away, glad you're goin' my way. I love it when we're
E
cruisin' together. The music is playin' for love,

To Coda
A
D
B
1
E
cruis - in' is made _ for love, _
I love _ it when we're cruis - in' to - geth - er.
2
E
N.C.
E
cruis - in' to - geth - er.
Cruise with me ba - by.
E
1-3
F♯m7
4
F♯m7
D.S. al Coda
(Instrumental solo ad lib./vocal ad lib.)
CODA
E
E
cruis - in' to - geth - er.
You're gon - na fly a - way, ___

A
D
B
glad you're go - in' my way.
I love it when we're
E
cruis - in' to - geth - er.
The mu - sic is playin' for love,
A
D
B
cruis - in' is made for love,
I love it when we're
Repeat and Fade
E
cruis - in' to - geth - er.
Optional Ending
E
cruis - in' to - geth - er.

GET READY

Words and Music by
WILLIAM "SMOKEY" ROBINSON

Dm
G
F
ev - er I'm asked who makes my dreams real I say that
lov - ing you're gon - na miss, and the time it takes to
hope I'll get to you be - fore they do, the way I
Dm
G
F
you do. (You're out - ta sight.) So
find you. (It's out - ta sight.) So
planned it. (Be out - ta sight.) So
Dm
G
F
fee fi, fo fum.
fid - dle - lee - dee, fid - dle - lee - dum.
twid - dle - dee - dee, twid - dle - dee - dum.
Dm
G
Look out, ba - by, 'cause here I come.

F
B♭
And I'm bring - ing you a love that's true so get
Gm7
3 fr
C7
C11
read - y, so get read - y.
F
B♭
I'm gon - na try to make love to you, so get
Gm7
3 fr
C7
C11
read - y, so get read - y, here I come.

Dm
1,2
G
F
I'm on my way.
Dm
If you
3
G
F
Dm
I'm on my way.
Dm
Repeat and Fade
G
Optional Ending
Dm
Get read - y, 'cause here I come, boy.

I SECOND THAT EMOTION

Words and Music by WILLIAM "SMOKEY" ROBINSON
and ALFRED CLEVELAND

may - be you'll go a - way and nev - er call, and a
may - be you think that love will make us fools, and
G
A
D
taste of hon - ey's worse than none at all.
so it makes you wise to break the rules.
Oh, lit - tle girl, in
G
D
that case I don't want no part. I do be - lieve that
G
D
that would on - ly break my heart. Oh, but

A
G
if you feel like lov-in' me, if you got the no - tion,
D
I sec - ond that e - mo - tion. So
A
G
if you feel like giv-ing me a life-time of de-vo - tion,
D
To Coda
I sec - ond that e - mo - tion.

1
A
G
May -
2
A
G
D
A
G
D.S. al Coda
Oh __ lit - tle girl __ in
CODA
A
G
D
Repeat ad lib. and Fade

MY GIRL

Words and Music by WILLIAM "SMOKEY" ROBINSON
and RONALD WHITE

F
C
Dm7
F
G
I guess you'll say,
C
Dm7
F
G
Cmaj9
what can make me feel this way?
My girl, (my girl,)
Dm7
To Coda
(my girl,) talk - in' 'bout my girl.
3
C/D
G7
Dm7
G
C
(My girl.) I've got so much

F
C
hon - ey, the bees en - vy me.
F
C
I've got a sweet - er song
F
C
F
D.S. al Coda
than the birds in the trees.
Well,
CODA
C/D
G7
Dm7
G
C
(My girl.) Ooh, hoo.

F
C
(Hey, hey, hey.)
F
Dm7
(Hey, hey, hey.)
G
Em
Ooh,
hoo,
yeah.

A
D
I don't need no mon - ey,
G
D
for - tune, or fame.
G
D
I've got all the rich - es, ba - by,
G
D
G
one man can claim.
Well,

D
Em7
G
A
D
Em7
I guess you'll say, what can make me
G
A
Dmaj9
4fr
feel this way?
My girl, (my girl,)
Em7
(my girl,) talk - in' 'bout my girl.
3
3
A
G
Dmaj7/F♯
Em
Dmaj9
4fr
(My girl.) (Talk - in' 'bout my girl,
I've got sun - shine on a
3
3

Em7
whoa __ whoa.) ______
cloud - y day __ with my girl; ______ I've
A G Dmaj7/F♯ Em Dmaj9
4 fr
(Talk - in' 'bout my girl, my girl,
e - ven got the month _ of May with my girl. ______
Em7
my girl, whoa __ whoa.) ______
Talk - in' 'bout, __ talk - in' 'bout, talk-in' 'bout _ my __ girl. ____
3
Repeat and Fade
A G Dmaj7/F♯ Em
(Talk - in' 'bout
Optional Ending
A G Dmaj7/F♯ Em Dmaj9
4 fr

MY GUY

Words and Music by
WILLIAM "SMOKEY" ROBINSON

Cm
F6
Cm
F6
Cm
F6
stick - ing to my guy like a stamp to a let - ter, like birds of a feath - er we
gave my guy my word of hon - or to be faith - ful,
Cm
B♭
B♭maj7
stick to - geth - er. I'm tell - in' you from the start I can't
and I'm gon - na. You best be be - liev - ing I won't
C7
F6
B♭
be torn a - part from my guy.
be de - ceiv - ing my guy.
1
Cm
Dm
2
Cm
Dm
Cm7
F
As a mat - ter of o - pin - ion I

Cm
F
Cm
F
B♭
think he's tops. My o-pin-ion is he's the cream of the crop. As a
Gm/F
Dm
Gm/F
Dm
C7
mat-ter of taste to be ex-act he's my i-deal as a
F7
B♭maj7
B♭6
B♭maj7
B♭6
mat-ter of fact. No mus-cle-bound man could take my hand from my
B♭maj7
B♭6
B♭maj7
B♭6
B♭maj7
B♭6
guy. (My guy.) No hand-some face could ev-er

B♭maj7
B♭6
Dm
D7
take the place of my guy.
(My guy.)
He
Cm
F
Cm
F
Cm
F
may not be a movie star, but when it comes to bein' happy
Cm
To Coda
B♭
Gm
C7
F7
3fr
we are. There's not a man today who could take me away from my
B♭maj7
B♭6
Cm
Dm
B♭
guy.

D.S. al Coda
Cm
3 fr
Dm
No
3
CODA
B♭
Gm
3 fr
C7
F7
man to - day who could take me a - way from my
B♭maj7
B♭6
Repeat and Fade
Cm
3 fr
Dm
guy.
(What you say, tell me more.)
there's not a
Optional Ending
Cm
3 fr
Dm
B♭
(Instrumental)

OOO BABY BABY

Words and Music by WILLIAM "SMOKEY" ROBINSON
and WARREN MOORE

Am7
Gmaj7
1
Am7
baby. Ooo, baby baby baby. Mis -
2,3
Am7
Gmaj7
baby. Ooo, baby
Ooo, baby
Am7
Gmaj7
To Coda
baby. Ooo, ooo, baby baby, I'm just a -
baby. Ooo, baby
Bm7
2fr
D11
bout at the end of my rope. But I can't stop

Bm7
2fr
D11
try - in', I can't give up hope 'cause I feel
G
Am7
some-day I'll hold you near. Whis - per I still
Bm7
2fr
Am7
D.S. al Coda
love you un - til that day is here. Ooo, I'm
CODA
Am7
Gmaj9
ba - by. Ooo.
rit.

QUIET STORM

Words and Music by WILLIAM "SMOKEY" ROBINSON
and ROSE ELLA JONES

dawn,
cane.
A pow - er
Luck - y
source
me,
of ten - der force.
um - brel - la free,
gen - er -
sud - den -
ate and ra - di - ate and turn me on,
ly I'm caught up in your sum - mer rain.
turn me
on.
La

Bm7
2fr
Bm7♭5
You short cir - cuit all my nerves.
Show-er me with your sweet love;
Hail soft storms of love on me;
Amaj9
Prom-is - ing e - lec - tric things,
you touch me and
I will bathe in ev - 'ry drop;
through all the sea - sons
Let then play on my de - sire.
(Kiss me soft - ly.)
Bm7♭5
sud-den - ly there's rain - bow rings.
Qui-et storm
let it pour and nev - er stop.
Let your light - ning light my fire.
Qui - et storm
Amaj9
Bm7/A
blow - ing
through my life,
blow - ing
through my life,

Amaj9
Bm7/A
Oh,
quiet storm
through my life, you're just like a quiet
Amaj9
Bm7/A
blow - ing
through my
storm
blow - ing
through my life.
Amaj9
Bm7/A
To Coda
life.
Oh,
1
Amaj9
blow ba - by.
Ah.
When you

2
Amaj9
(Instrumental)
D.S. al Coda
CODA
Amaj9
Repeat and Fade
Optional Ending
Blow ba - by.

OPEN

Words and Music by PAMELA MOFFETT-YOUNG,
MARVIN TARPLIN and WILLIAM "SMOKEY" ROBINSON

G7 F F♯ G Bb/G C/G G7 F F♯ G
no more closed in feel - in's. Ooh,
Gm Gm/F Gm/Bb C(add9) Gm Gm/F
3 fr
all the signs are flash - in', a warm de - sire, the wel-come mat is out for you to
Gm/Bb C(add9) G Bb/G C/G G7 F F♯ G
come and in - spire.
(O - pen.)
G Bb/G C/G G7 F F♯ G
O - pen, you don't have to

G
Bb/G
C/G
G7
F
F#
G
knock to come in,
and let love be - gin.
G7
Bb/G
C/G
G7
F
F#
G
Yeah,
un - fold - ed arms are
G
Bb/G
C/G
G7
F
F#
G
o - pened
to em - brace your
G
Bb/G
C/G
G7
F
F#
G
bod - y
with all the hold - in'

G Bb/G C/G G7 F F# G
two arms can give for as long as we live.
G7 Bb/G C/G G F F# G
Yeah, want you to know that
Gm Gm/F Gm/Bb C(add9)
3 fr
just hav - in' you; that is the key
Gm Gm/F Gm/Bb C(add9)
3 fr
to what's been locked up in - side of me. O -

Gm
3 fr
pen.
(O - pen.)
Hey, oh, yeah, ooh.
Gm
3 fr
Gm/F
Gm/B♭
C(add9)
G
B♭/G
C/G
O - pen, ooh,
O - pen,

G7
F
F#
G
G
Bb/G
C/G
my mind is hold - in' o - pen house.
my love for you is o - pen, well.
G7
F
F#
G
G
Bb/G
C/G
Sug-ges - tions that you're read - y to make,
And all the stops can now be - come go
G
F
F#
G
G7
Bb/G
C/G
oh, I'm read - y to take. Oh, yeah.
if you make it so. Oh, yeah.
1
G7
F
F#
G
Oh,
2
G7
F
F#
G
Tell 'em 'bout a - hav - in'

Gm
Gm/F
Gm/B♭
C(add9)
3 fr
just hav - in' you;
that is the key
to what's been locked up in - side of me.
You got me
G
B♭/G
C/G
G7
F
F♯
o - pen.
Well,
ev - 'ry - thing is
o - pen.
Ev - 'ry-thing
and ev - 'ry - thing that

G
B♭/G
C/G
G7
F
F♯
G
I wan - na do
is de-pend - ing on you.
G7
B♭/G
C/G
G
F
F♯
G
Oh, don't you know that my life is wide
Repeat and Fade
G
B♭/G
C/G
G7
F
F♯
G
o - pen.
(Well, well, well.)
Optional Ending
G7
F
F♯
G
rit.

SHOP AROUND

Words and Music by BERRY GORDY
and WILLIAM "SMOKEY" ROBINSON

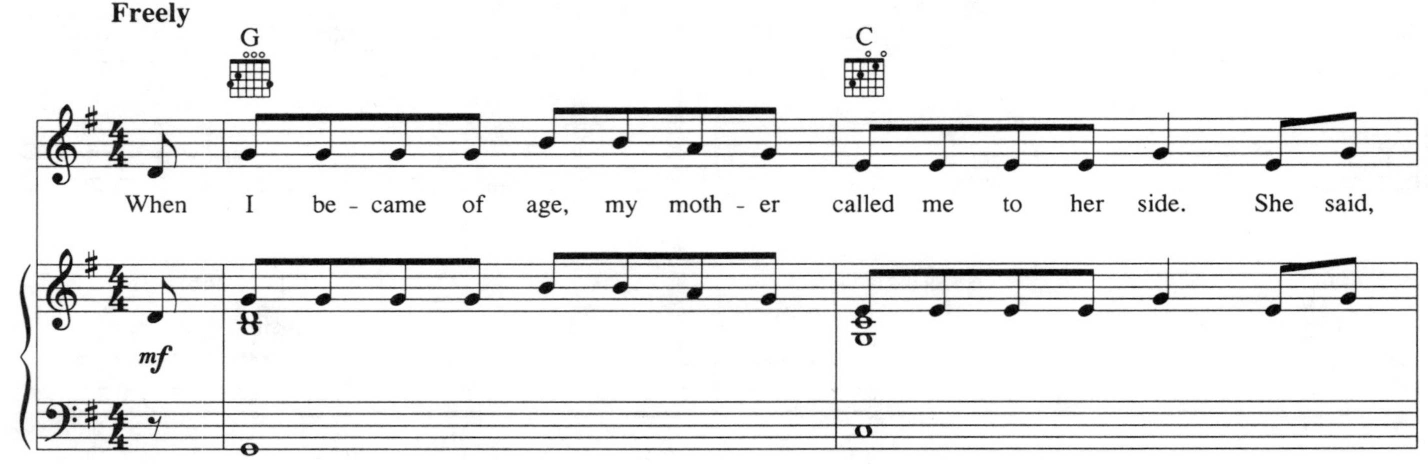

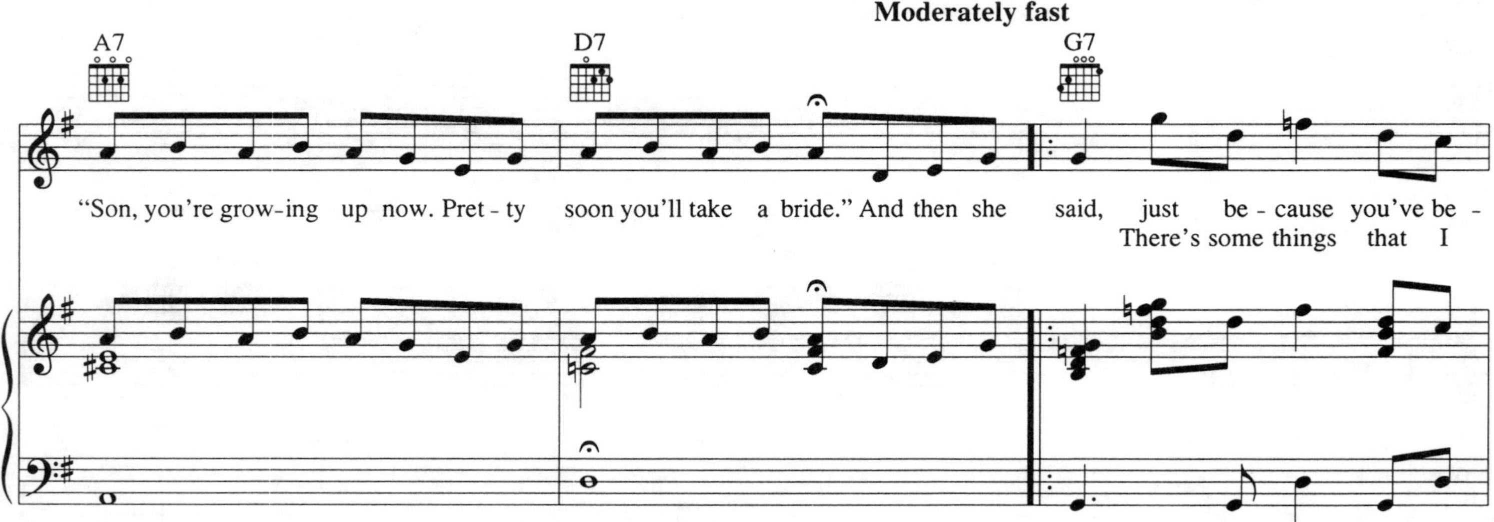

C7
G7
C7
don't un - der - stand now. Be - fore you ask some girl for her hand now,
wind's gon - na blow now, the wom - en come and the wom - en gon - na go now.
G7
C7
A7
keep your free - dom for as long as you can now.
Be - fore you tell 'em that you love 'em so now,
My ma - ma told
D7
N.C.
G7
C7
me you bet - ter shop a - round, oh yeah, you bet - ter shop a -
G7
1
D7
round. Ah

2
D7
C7
Try to get your - self a
G7
bar - gain, son. Don't be sold on the ver - y first one.
C7
A7
N.C.
Pret - ty girls come a dime a doz - en. A - try to find one who's gon - na
D7
N.C.
G7
C7
give you true lov - in'. Be - fore you take a girl and say I do now,

G7
C7
To Coda
A7
make sure she's in love with ___ you now. My ma - ma told
D7
N.C.
G7
me you bet - ter shop a - round.
3
C7
G7
C7
G7
C7

G7
D.S. al Coda
CODA
G7
C7
G7
Make sure that her love is true now.
I hate to see you feel-in'
C7
A7
D7
N.C.
sad and blue now.
My ma-ma told me
you bet-ter shop a-
G7
C7
Repeat and Fade
round.

THE TEARS OF A CLOWN

Words and Music by STEVIE WONDER,
WILLIAM "SMOKEY" ROBINSON and HENRY COSBY

C♭ G♭ D♭ G♭ C♭ G♭
now hon - ey that's quite a dif-f'rent sub - ject. Don't
to cov - er this hurt with a show of glad - ness. But don't
D♭ G♭ C♭ G♭ D♭ G♭
let my glad ex - pres - sion give you the wrong im - pres -
let my show con - vince you that I've been hap - py since
C♭ G♭ D♭ G♭ C♭ G♭
- sion; real - ly I'm sad, Oh, sad - der than sad,
you de - cid - ed to go, I need you so,
D♭ G♭ C♭ G♭ D♭ G♭
you're gone and I'm hurt - ing so bad, like a clown,
I'm hurt and I want you to know, but for oth -

Cb Gb Db Gb Cb Gb
I pre - tend to be glad.
- ers I put on a show.
Now there's some
Ab 4fr F/A Bbm
sad things known to man but ain't too much sad - der than
Gbmaj7 Db N.C.
the tears of a clown, when there's no one a -
round.
1
Db Gb

Cb Gb Db Gb Cb Gb
Oh yeah,
Now, if I ap - pear
2
Db Gb Cb Gb Db Gb
Just like Pag - li - ac - ci did,
I try to keep my sad -
Cb Gb Db Gb Cb Gb
- ness hid,
smil - ing in the pub - lic eye
but in my
Db Gb Cb Gb Db
N.C.
lone - ly room I cry the tears of a clown,

Additional Lyrics

Now, if there's a smile on my face
Don't let my glad expression
Give you a wrong impression
Don't let this smile I wear
Make you think that I don't care *(Fade)*

YOU'VE REALLY GOT A HOLD ON ME

Words and Music by
WILLIAM "SMOKEY" ROBINSON

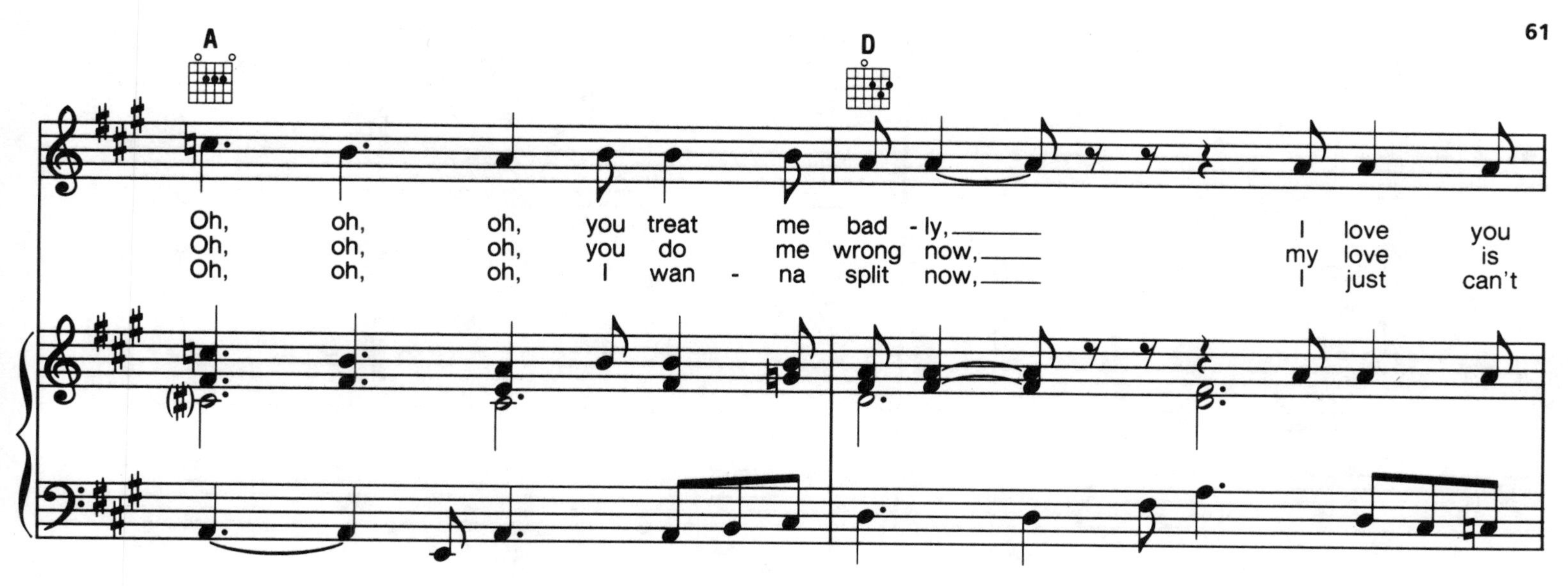
A
D
Oh, oh, oh, you treat me bad - ly,
Oh, oh, oh, you do me wrong now,
Oh, oh, oh, I wan - na split now,
I love you
my love is
I just can't

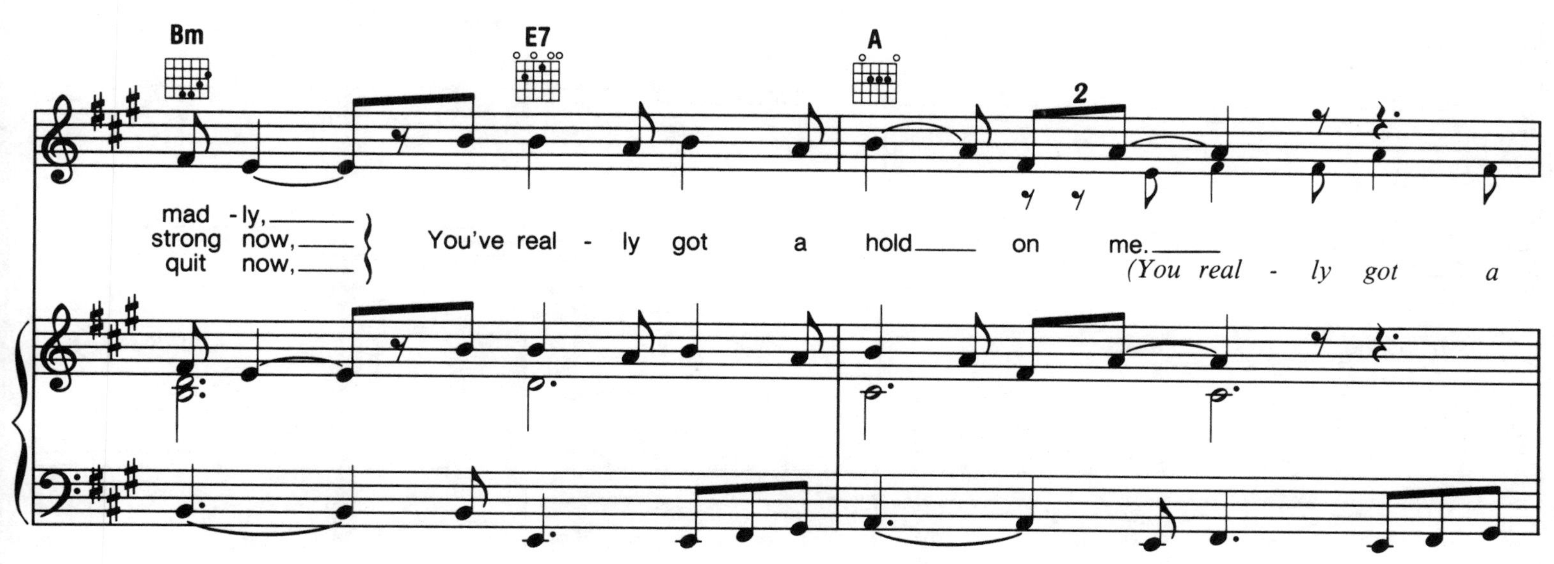
Bm
E7
A
2
mad - ly,
strong now,
quit now,
You've real - ly got a hold on me.
(You real - ly got a

1
F♯m
You real - ly got a hold on me.
Ba - by,
hold on me.)
(You real - ly got a hold on me.)

2,3
F♯m
hold on me.
(You real - ly got a hold on me.)
Ba - by,
A
A7
D
I love you and all I want you to do is just
A
E7
To Coda
1. hold me, hold me, hold me, hold me.
2. hold me, (please) hold me, (squeeze) hold me, hold me.
A
F♯m
E
A
Tight - er

F♯m
E
A
D.S. al Coda
Tight - er!
CODA
A
You real - ly got a hold on me,
(You real - ly got a hold on me.)
F♯m
You real - ly got a hold on me.
(You real - ly got a hold on me.)
A